Praise for *Slices o*

"*Slices of Life* began at age eight, when the author was given a diary and discovered her true purpose in life: to chronicle events and be a storyteller. ...Packed with impressions, sounds, tastes, and scenes...readers who love warm family memories are in for a treat."

    –D. DONOVAN, *Midwest Book Review*

"I am in love with Ann Nyberg's stories. With every vividly painted chapter, I recalled a memory of my own, which I think, is exactly what she planned. Her storytelling triggers the reader to remember the slices of their own lives, the precious moments that sometimes pass too quickly. And, isn't that what life is really all about. Thank you Ann, for taking me to those cherished times."

    –KITT SHAPIRO, devoted daughter of the late
    actress and singer, Eartha Kitt

"Ann Nyberg is a knitter. In *Slices of Life* she knits a warming life narrative of dandelion necklaces, mason jars and the simple pieces of life that prepared her for a heralded story-telling career. Ann's a daughter, wife, mother and friend who knows the value of a tale well told and she recounts many well in *Slices of Life*. Just ask Susan the waitress and make sure you're eating a cookie when you do."

    –PHIL LENGYEL, Ann's First News Director
    in Elkhart, Indiana and former Disney Executive

Slices of Life

a storyteller's diary

Slices of Life

a storyteller's diary

THIS DIARY BELONGS TO

Ann Nyberg

HOMEBOUND
PUBLICATIONS
Independent Publisher of Contemplative Titles
STONINGTON, CONNECTICUT

HOMEBOUND PUBLICATIONS

FIRST EDITION TRADE PAPERBACK
ISBN: 978-1-938846-51-9 (pbk)

Visit the publisher at www.homeboundpublications.com or visit the author
at Ann Nyberg's Network Connecticut www.networkconnecticut.com

Book Designed by Leslie M. Browning
Cover and Interior Images © Ann Nyberg

Library of Congress Cataloging-in-Publication Data

Nyberg, Ann, 1957-
 Slices of life : a storyteller's diary / by Ann Nyberg. –First edition, trade
paperback.
   pages cm
 ISBN 978-1-938846-51-9 (paperback)
 1. Nyberg, Ann, 1957- 2. Nyberg, Ann, 1957—Childhood and youth. 3.
Nyberg, Ann, 1957—Philosophy. 4. Storytelling–Philosophy. 5. Conduct
of life–Philosophy. 6. Women television news anchors–Connecticut–New
Haven–Biography. 7. Television news anchors–Connecticut–New Haven-
-Biography. I. Title.
 PN4913.N92A3 2015
 070.1'95092--dc23
 [B]
                                                          2015013838

10 9 8 7 6 5 4 3 2 1

Homebound Publications greatly values the natural environment
and invests in environmental conservation. Our books are printed
on paper with chain of custody certification from the Forest Stew-
ardship Council, Sustainable Forestry Initiative, and the Program
for the Endorsement of Forest Certification. In addition, each year
Homebound Publications donates 1% of our net profit to a hu-
manitarian or ecological charity. To learn more about this year's

charity visit www.homeboundpublications.com

Acknowledgments

Thanks to all my family and friends for giving me the life I have and to everyone who has ever told me a story.

To my husband Mark, our children, Lindsay, Sarah, Katie and son-in-law, Paul and our beloved pets, Pepsi, Savannah Jane, Henry Watson, and Mr. Trip Meeshu, I cherish the memories we continue to make.

To all of my TV news colleagues with whom I've worked over the years at WSJV-TV, KOCO-TV, KFOR-TV, and WTNH-TV, where I saddled up to the news desk in January of 1987, it has been a privilege to be on deadline with all of you. A debt of gratitude to the guy who gave me my start in television journalism, my first News Director, Phil Lengyel.

And finally my heartfelt thanks to my publisher, author Leslie M. Browning for giving me the chance to be a published author.

Contents

About the Author

About the Press

Introduction

I've been a storyteller all my life; that's just who I am. When I was eight years old, my mom gave me a diary for Christmas. That was the beginning of a life of writing. I had a need to document things—all kinds of things—appointments, what the weather was like, anything and everything. I wrote about relatives coming over to our house and what we did, and on and on and on. As a teenager, I kept copious notes about babysitting: who the children were, how long the job lasted, and how much money I made, (which, let's face it, it wasn't a lot when you were getting 50 cents an hour back in the 1970's, but it was something). I even recorded the dates I had with boys in high school. I wish I could find that gem of a book, but those chapters were lost over time.

Yes, I was always writing, keeping track of my life, preserving the past so that I can remember things—big and small. I never ever thought about putting some of my stories into a book. But, after a chance meeting with a Connecticut author, I decided to start writing and see what I could come up with. Enter Leslie Browning, founder of Homebound Publications, who said, "I'll publish it." And, that's how this book found its way into the world. You just never know what might happen in life. And heck, now I have a bunch of my stories all in one place. I have a storyteller's diary.

As I was writing, I realized just how important these stories are to me, especially the stories about my family. I can leave something behind for my kids and my grandkids. Through these pages, I can tell them stories about what happened during my lifetime. I can share the lessons that I learned. There is something to learn from everything that happens in one's life. Those lessons are contained in stories—both good and bad stories.

I've been chronicling slices of my life from the time I could talk. I love learning about the particulars of an event or story first so I could tell everybody else. It's no surprise that I chose journalism as my profession. Becoming a television reporter seemed so natural; I had been doing my own kind of reporting at an amateur level for years. I had been given a little camera as a youngster and took the most photos in my family. I was a very visual person, so television news was perfect—reporting stories with pictures.

In June of 1979, I took a job as a television news reporter in Elkhart, Indiana, near South Bend, where I grew up. That was about a month after I graduated from Purdue University. I was off and running on a "professional" level, and the rest is history, as they say. My first story was about a lion cub at a mall. Yep, I started out pretty hard-hitting. I still have that story in a box somewhere down in the basement on a reel of film. I've been "on the air" from Indiana to Oklahoma to Connecticut, either behind the news desk or out in the field letting folks know what's going on in their backyards. Along the way, I have learned that people are pretty much the same everywhere; that they need and want respect, and that acts of kindness go a long way in the world. In the end, it's the simple pleasures we hold dear. I was raised to think about others and help whenever possible.

At present, I think we're living in a pretty narcissistic, all-about-me world. I don't like it, and it doesn't lead to a strong culture or country. Things are out of whack. Greed has grown to new heights. I am very troubled about what this is teaching our children.

Our society is falling apart in many ways. We live in a world in which pop culture makes a headline while the lemonade stand down the street, where children are raising money for cancer research, goes unnoticed. What do you do about all of this? The answer: roll up your sleeves and teach those around you about civility; how to say "please" and "thank you" and "excuse me." My grammy Waggoner used to say, "Mind your P's and Q's".

The generations coming up behind you may not even know a may-I-help-you kind of life. Customer service went out the window somewhere along the way, and that's key to getting us back on track as a society. The get-it-yourself, never-talk-to-a-live-person-on-the-phone mentality is maddening. I was born in 1957, things were different then, not all good of course, but there was more civility around, I just know there was. Because of technology, we live in a connected-yet-disconnected world.

We need to figure out how to start having conversations again—real conversations, meaningful conversations.

You may or may not have experienced the kinds of things I've written about. Your age will likely have something to do with your ability to relate to these stories. I do hope that you find some valuable lessons in this book. As you read, I invite you to think about your own life and cherish the things you have learned. Your stories make you who you are. I then encourage you to write your stories down for others. You'll learn so much about yourself in the process.

So, these are some of the stories of my life. I hope that you enjoy them. They made me who I am: a storyteller, one who grew up to tell your stories on the evening news. It is my hope that this book will inspire you to see the splendor in a blue sky, contemplate weeds in a field as flowers, engage in meaningful conversation with those around you, and help others when you can.

—Ann Nyberg
Connecticut, Spring 2014

My Early Beginnings

I was born in a Quonset hut on Goodfellow Air Force Base in San Angelo, Texas on January 23, 1957. My dad, Captain John W. Nyberg, Jr., was a pilot. He and Mom were young twenty-somethings serving the nation. I have often thought about my humble beginnings in Texas. I've searched for photos of that makeshift hospital on the airbase, but have yet to find one. I do consider myself a "research queen" who leaves no stone unturned, so I should be up to the task of finding a shot of the actual place of my birth. My mom reminds me her military obstetrician made up for the no-big-deal room in which I emerged. She has told me over and over again, for decades how remarkably handsome her obstetrician was. I wonder if I should try to track him down too along with a photo of my Quonset hut. Have you ever seen a Quonset hut?

Wikipedia describes it as, "a lightweight prefabricated structure of corrugated galvanized steel having a semicircular cross-section." Sounds special doesn't it? In the late 1950's, these were the kind of dwellings erected on military bases. They went up fast and could come down just as quickly.

At the time of my birth, President Dwight D. Eisenhower, the nations' 34th Commander-in-Chief, made a visit to the airbase; that's what you called "big doings." I was lying there in that bassinet, less than a week old, while the President of the United States was nearby, chatting it up and rubbing elbows with military brass.

After San Antonio bootcamp, my dad earned his pilot wings at Graham Air Force Base in Marianna, Florida. He flew all kinds of planes in the Air Force, including the B-47 Bomber. He frequently told the story about the time he, as a navigator, was involved in a crash landing on an airbase. He wasn't hurt physically—he and the crew got very lucky—but that accident shook him to his core. Although he did travel on commercial flights years later, he much preferred to be on a plane that allowed him to have a parachute strapped to his back.

My mom, Ellen Deane Waggoner Nyberg, married Dad on August 13, 1955. They spent three years in the Air Force, hopping from base to base with me and, eventually, my sister, Sue Ellen.

*   *   *

Mom and Dad met at Central High School in South Bend. My dad went off to Indiana University and my mother to Ball State University. After a year, they decided they missed each other too much and she transferred to I.U..

My mom's middle name, Deane, came from her Dad's mom, Cordelia Deane. How's that for an old-fashioned name? Her gram's nickname was "Cordie." I only knew her for a little while, but I do remember she always had M&M's in a candy dish on a table. I loved that.

My mom's first name, Ellen, came from a narrative poem, *The Lady of the Lake*, written in 1810 by Sir Walter Scott. The story, featured in Scotland, had a heroine in it by the name of Ellen Douglass. My grandfather, Chester Waggoner, talked my grandmother into naming their first child, Ellen. Funny how people pick names isn't it? The story goes that my grandfather read *The Lady of the Lake* during the two years he was a student at Purdue University. He didn't graduate from Purdue though; instead he went back home and worked in the family business. Many years later, I would attend Purdue and, yes, graduate with a degree in Journalism.

My sister, Sue Ellen, is eighteen months younger than I am. She was born at Dyess Air Force Base in Abilene, Texas. Her "birth digs" were much better than mine, and her military hospital was beautiful. Okay, whatever.

To take a moment to round out the rest of the siblings for you, who were not military brats: John William Nyberg III was born five years after Sue Ellen, in Indianapolis, Indiana, where my dad went to dental school at Indiana University. (I never heard how John's hospital was, though I know it was modern.)

Nine years after I was born my sister, Carol Hope came along. She was born in South Bend, Indiana, where my folks grew up. I remember my dad's parents came over to babysit us kids while Carol was being delivered. I vividly recall passing my mom on the stairs in our house as she was headed down to the main floor on her way to the hospital. She didn't say much. She was in labor and on a mission, which I totally get now having had three children of my own, including twins.

South Bend is the place we grew up, for the most part. We lived 90 miles east of Chicago, Illinois, in the shadow of the golden dome of the University of Notre Dame, just like my folks had.

As kids, we loved to go to restaurants that had booths. I always felt "hugged" by them. Who doesn't like that feeling of being snug and cozy when dining out? It never mattered to me that the naugahyde could be cold, or that your legs stuck to it in the hot summer months. It felt like home to me; the furniture in our family room was all naugahyde. We had a big red naugahyde easy chair and a chartreuse naugahyde hide-a-bed sofa. My mother loved this furniture because kids couldn't destroy it. It took a beating and yet continued to look brand new. You just can't destroy naugahyde, which of course, is why you find it in diners.

Sometimes the naugahyde would get polished with Pledge and that would make the furniture slick. We then figured out what fun it was to slide off the cushions. We created a game of it.

So that's a brief, early history of my family. It gives you an idea of who I am, where I came from, and how I ended up the way I did. There was a good bit of humor injected into my childhood. Boy, is that important.

*   *   *

All of us are just passing through. It matters how you live your life. You have one shot at it. It matters how you treat people, what you do for others…the little things that become huge over a lifetime.

At 57, I have adopted a live-with-urgency kind of mentality; you have to live life to its fullest because you never know what is around the corner. A friend of mine, Mary Ann Wasil lives this way after battles with cancer. Mary Ann believes you have to, "live a full life no matter what and always take stock of what's going on around you." Don't waste time on silly things or silly people. Everybody says "life is short," because it is. My sister, Carol, was diagnosed with breast cancer, and so was my cousin Margaret. Both are heroes to me, as are the countless other women who go up against this dreaded disease. Carol and Margaret fought it valiantly. They emerged as compassionate guides to anyone else facing similar challenges.

The following chapters are about things that matter to me; maybe they will matter to you too, or get you thinking in new directions.

Perhaps, these stories will serve as reminders of what's important. With age comes wisdom. No, really, that's true.

Your life's beginnings is the start of your story.
—Ann Nyberg

Simple Times

As I start to take stock of the life I have lived for nearly sixty years, I find myself focusing more and more on early childhood memories. I guess, everyone does.

I went to kindergarten at School 79 in Eagledale, Indiana, a section of Indianapolis. (The school didn't have a name, just a number.) I had my first crush at five years old, on a boy in the neighborhood who went to my school. His name was Jimmy Sullivan. Jimmy gave me a blue poodle pin made of rhinestones. Maybe he took it from his mom's jewelry box or maybe she bought it for him to give to me. I don't know, but I still wonder about its origins. I had the pin for a very long time. It was a treasure, one that I can't find now, which kind of makes me a little sad. I suspect that blue dog from Jimmy was what sparked my love affair with rhinestone jewelry, and glitter, and other things that sparkle. I do say that "glitter" is my favorite color!

Where is Jimmy these days and what has happened in his life? Sometimes I find myself reflecting on the movie we went to see one Saturday afternoon in the school gym. Does he remember the time we spent together playing in the sandbox? I've been married to my husband, Mark, for thirty-four years. He's had ample opportunity to tease me about my first—and longest lasting—crush.

Eagledale was a little "starter" neighborhood near the Indianapolis Motor Speedway. In the days leading up to the Indianapolis 500, around Memorial Day weekend, we would sit in the house and listen to the souped-up engines, as the cars raced around the track, and around again. We lived in a house that looked like the little square, plastic, green ones you find in the Monopoly game. Although the houses in our neighborhood were not all dark green, they were pretty much the same cookie-cutter design, straight out of the 1950's. Imagine match box race cars zooming around a Monopoly board. That was our life back then.

Dad was in dental school. I'll never figure out how flying and looking into someone's mouth go together, but that's where he ended up and he would go on to be a well-loved hometown dentist for the rest of his money-making years.

My siblings and I spent a good bit of time playing in the backyard with the neighborhood kids. Back then, that's just what you did—you played outside with other people. None of us had lots of toys. There were bicycles and balls and hula-hoops, stuff like that, but not much else. We didn't need more. There were adventures to be had, like the time fire ants invaded our backyard sandbox. Sue took the brunt of it that day. Oh, the bites she had! Tons of them.

One weekend my dad decided to gather the neighbors and cook eggs on the top of our 1957 Chevy. Those were the kind of silly, simple things we did for fun. First, we washed off the hood and made it all spick-and-span. As the temperature got to about 100 degrees Fahrenheit, on went the eggs. They cooked right up, in fine sunny-side up fashion right on the hood of the car. That was a pretty cool *Mr. Science* kind of thing to do. The neighborhood kids couldn't believe what was going on right before their eyes. I bet some of them still remember it.

*   *   *

In those days, nobody went to the beauty parlor. You did your own hair. That went for all the women in the neighborhood, as well as their kids. I had, and still have, poker-straight hair. No curl, ever, not even on days with 100 percent humidity.

Unfortunately that made me a perfect candidate for one of the very popular Toni Home Permanents. Yep, my mom curled my hair in the backyard. Looking back, it seems like it took hours to put that icky, strong-smelling solution stuff over the tiny pink curlers rolled tightly against my head. When my hair was washed and dried, I looked exactly like Shirley Temple—a mop of ringlet curls all over my head. I could have been a stand-in for Shirley in one of her movies. Picture me now: a curly-haired little girl in a matching light blue t-shirt and shorts made by Buster Brown. In those days, I pulled my elastic-waisted shorts right up to just under my chin. I couldn't stand to wear anything around my waist. I continued this practice until the age of eight or nine, when someone told me that wearing one's waistline at the neck level was not especially fetching. Okay, so maybe I wasn't a

Shirley Temple look-a-like, but I might have been willing to wear the shorts at my waist if someone had offered to give me a movie role. (That would have been great for my college fund.) Those days were really simple times. Does everyone who starts reflecting on their childhood feel that way? We didn't need a lot of material stuff to make us happy; the moms and dads raising their kids in my little "village" didn't have much money, and it didn't matter. But the best part of being a really little kid is that you don't care what other people think, you're just floating through life. You make up stories in your mind and play all day long. Those are some of the best days of one's life.

In 1963, we moved to South Bend, Indiana where I started first grade. That was the year that President John F. Kennedy was assassinated. It shattered the nation's innocence.

I remember that day clearly. I was at Webster Elementary School. There was some kind of an announcement in my red brick school building that spread like wildfire and the next thing I knew all the teachers were crying. All of the students were sent home. I didn't understand what was happening. I felt like I should be crying too because everyone else was. When I reached the house after my short walk home, I discovered my mom sitting in front of the television, crying. Walter Cronkite was on our black and white TV set. I became transfixed on the unfolding story about the death of our President. Two days later, I watched the President's funeral on TV. John-John saluted his father's casket as it rolled by. This had a huge impact on me.

Cronkite was at the CBS helm, guiding us through those dark days. In my 40's, I met Cronkite. He was "the most trusted man in America." I interviewed him about his life at Southern Connecticut State University. We sat on stage talking for more than an hour, in front of a big crowd. I had felt a lot of self-imposed pressure going into the interview, but once I got started, the questions flowed. The relationship flowed. It was such a joy to be able to chat with him and learn from his life story. That may have been the highlight of my professional career.

> *The innocence of childhood is precious.*
> *We need to remember that as an adult.*
> —Ann Nyberg

Four-leaf Clovers and Dandelion Necklaces

My mom could find a four-leaf clover like a heat-seeking missile can find its target. It was uncanny. Whether we were in someone's backyard or just out for a walk, if there was a four-leaf clover to be found, she'd find it. She'd drop to her knees and pluck it right out of the ground for all to see. I saw this happen repeatedly, but it was always a surprise. She wouldn't say that she was looking for one but there it was, suddenly taken up in her hand. The little clover was always carried home from wherever she found it and put in a drinking glass or dish in the kitchen. This was her proud trophy—an award for the day's doings. I have since been told that my mom's mother, my grammy Waggoner, was equally gifted with "the luck." My cousin, Margaret, too. But, Mom was the master.

At the time, most of the family didn't realize how precious Mom's four-leaf clover skills were, but she knew it was something special. I now realize how this ability set her apart. She never boasted about her finds. She's a caring, compassionate woman. Mom taught us well and is still our teacher to this day.

Mom remembers the clover patch in the backyard of her childhood home on Sherman Avenue in South Bend. She suspects that patch was full of four-leaf clovers. I have never heard of such a thing—a patch of clovers in which all would have four leaves. Hogwash. But, then again, who knows? I've only found one or two of these rare little treasures in my life. Maybe I need to visit that patch.

When Mom was in a high school club called, "The Spurs" she made a cake and decorated it with four-leaf clovers—*real* four-leaf clovers! No one does that, but she did. Are there pictures of this? There was magic at work, real magic.

The clover plant gives rise to little white flowers. My mom delighted in showing me and Sue how to make clover bracelets and clover necklaces like she had made with her mom as a child. She would gather up the flower stalks and knot the stems just so, all in one direction. They would come out perfectly. You can't pull too hard on the stems or they'll break. You have to have a gentle touch. This jewelry from nature is a part of my childhood.

Dandelion flowers work too. I guess that's why I don't consider clover or dandelions to be weeds. They are flowers to me.

When my oldest daughter, Lindsay, was just a wee one, we lived right next to a Christmas tree farm. We were in Hamden, Connecticut, and the field in which those trees grew had more than its fair share of dandelions. We collected them and put them in little vases around the house. Cost efficient, you bet. Lovely, yes. There are many stages of beauty in a dandelion. When the flowers are gone, they turn into a wispy transparent lollipop. That's a great source of playtime for children too; spending hours blowing dandelion seeds into the wind. I have a photo of Lindsay in the dandelion patch, seemingly without a care in the world, wind in her hair, just being a kid. It's a favorite.

Queen Anne's Lace holds special memories too. There were acres of that beautiful plant around my grandfather Waggoner's dairy farm—fields for as far as the eye could see during the summer months. That flower is best left in the ground. If you put it in a vase, it sure doesn't last very long. It's just meant to be in fields.

> *The luck of the Irish isn't just for the Irish,*
> *it's for Ellen too.*
> —Ann Nyberg

> *Dandelions are only weeds if you see them that way.*
> *Look beyond the flowers to the memories.*
> —Ann Nyberg

Mason Jar Love

What is it about a simple, little mason jar that we love so much? It's been around, seemingly forever in a variety of colors—clear, blue, green. It serves as a vase, a drinking glass, a container to hold a myriad of precious things.

I suppose most people think of the mason jar as a jam or jelly jar. There is a ritual to boiling and sealing the glasses packed with fresh summer fruit, sugar, and pectin to enjoy in the cold winter months. That said, I've never actually *canned* anything. My daughter Katherine Elizabeth—known to the family as Katie or Kates—has made jam several times. Katie is five minutes younger than her twin sister, Sarah. We constantly beg her to run a restaurant. Night after night, she turns out fantastic dishes in our kitchen. She could be a chef anywhere. Katie and my husband, Mark, pickle peppers too. They use a recipe passed down from Mark's dad. Emil passed away in December of 2013, at the age of 91.

Emil was quite a guy, a U.S. Marine who served in the South Pacific. He and my mother-in-law were married for more than 60 years. They had many things in common, including "tripping the light fantastic." They loved to dance. And, he had a brain for problem solving. There wasn't anything that he couldn't figure out. My husband is much the same man. Am I lucky, or what?

The mason jar was front and center during the Great Depression, when everybody had the so-called "Victory Garden." People went back to basics, growing and preserving their own produce. The most recent time in which everybody went back to basics was in 2008, the Great Recession in the U.S. and around the world. We started thinking again about living simply and saving money. What if we all chose to live this way, whether or not the country is in a depression? How might the world change?

Since 2008, mason jars have made a comeback. They are everywhere. They're not only used for canning, but also as ice tea glasses in restaurants, containers for candles, vases for flowers at weddings, whatever the imagination wishes. I used a lot of antique blue mason jars when Lindsay married our beyond-wonderful son-in-law, Paul. They met at the University of Connecticut. Lindsay loved the look of the mason jars on the tables, and so did everyone else. That jar stands for the "basics" and that's how I grew up. Something borrowed. Something blue.

I subscribe to the make-do-use-what-you-have method of decorating. When the so-called "Shabby Chic" décor came into fashion, my approach to decorating was suddenly all the rage—and expensive for those who couldn't do it yourself! I've always looked for the good in something old and painted it, or rehabbed it, reused, and repurposed. Yep, got it. Nobody should ever live beyond their means. It is important to save for a rainy day. These are things you and I have heard for generations. Take it to the bank. Live by these sayings.

At my grammy Waggoner's house, I used to drink water out of an aluminum two cup capacity measuring cup. Because it was metal, it kept the water really, really cold. Not many of the glasses in her kitchen cupboard matched, but I liked it that way; you got to select a different glass every time you needed one. I think my gram was an early, Martha Stewart. Martha doesn't match things. Have you seen some of the tables she sets with all different kinds of dishes and glasses? The chairs don't match either. I love that. Simpler is better. Use what you have. It's more interesting that way.

Look no further than a mason jar
for all your needs.
—Ann Nyberg

Humor is Important, Remember That!

Nobody understands my childhood like my sisters and brother. In the early days, we lived in a world all our own, in a two story house, in a neighborhood where there weren't many kids. But, we had each other. We all had an imagination that ran wild. Thankfully, it ran wild in the same direction. We dreamed up stories—a lot of stories. Since I was the oldest, most of the stories were my ideas. The others helped decide how we would act the stories out. To this day, we all share this weird, creative humor. You ought to be in the room with the four of us sometime, you'd have a ball.

Our mom was a stay-at-home mom and for a while we only had one car, Dad took it to work. He had the daunting task of running his own dental office while raising four kids. He worked long hours and on the weekends too. He missed many of our performances. The house—all of it—was our stage. The yard was fair game too and so were all the neighbors' yards—everything. We did our best to engage everything and everyone in our imaginary day-to-day plays. We all had—and have—a quirky sense of humor and can make each other laugh in a heartbeat.

We dreamed up many scenarios over the years. I'll recap a few of our antics for you. We may be spread across the country these days, but we remain connected through memory and humor. I am in Connecticut; Sue is near South Bend, in Mishawaka; John is in Madison, Indiana; and Carol is in Kennesaw, Georgia.

The house we grew up in was on Myrtle Avenue. It was a plain white colonial with black shutters. To the left of our house was a 1960's ranch. That's where Mr. and Mrs. Smeeten lived. We loved saying their name out loud. It never failed to make us laugh. We'd say, "Smeeten, Smeeten, Smeeten." To this day, we talk about that name and giggle.

The Smeetens were real characters. For some reason, Mr. Smeeten always had tons of plastic phonebook covers, in many different colors, with advertising all over them. They were stored in his garage in boxes. As a result of whatever it was Mr. Smeeten did for a living, all of us kids benefited. He gave us as many covers as we wanted. As a kid, you can create something out of virtually anything, and that's what we did with those phonebook covers. They were a prized toy. Imagine that! Just a piece of plastic that covered a book, that's it. We would put them around notebooks, cut them up and make little tablecloths for the Barbie house, use them to cover spy manuscripts that we made up. They had a million and one uses.

Mrs. Smeeten was a homemaker, like my mom, but older. She looked like actress, Agnes Moorehead when she played the role of Endora, in the 1960's comedy hit TV show *Bewitched*. *Bewitched* was very popular in our house. We used to twitch our noses pretending that we too could create magic. Mrs. Smeeten, in our eyes, looked and dressed like the character. Mrs. Smeeten loved to wear brightly-colored kaftans just like Endora and she even had the character's bouffanted red hair too. Oh yes,

Mrs. Smeeten was a hoot to look at and to watch. On the other hand, Mr. Smeeten was nondescript. I have no recollection of what he looked like, except that he didn't have much hair. Funny what you take notice of as kids.

One day the Smeetens had a garden hose problem. It turned into a huge deal. (I am giggling as I am writing this because this was big doings in the neighborhood or at least we thought so as kids.)

Mrs. Smeeten turned the water on and, somehow, the ground started eating her hose, sucking it further and further down into the ground until it ripped itself right off the house. Yes, water started shooting out everywhere! This, of course, caused panic. She started screaming for help, flapping her arms, her flowing kaftan waving. We heard the screams and darted out of the house to observe the chaos. Maybe it was a sinkhole. I don't know. At some point, my dad helped rectify things. Where was Mr. Smeeten? I don't know.

Imagination is so important for kids—essential really—and I worry that children aren't using their imagination much anymore. Playing outside has turned to playing games online inside—doing what others have made up for them—rather than creating their own adventures. Parents need to figure out how to get their kids to unplug and enjoy the things around them.

A life without imagination is pretty darn dull.
—Ann Nyberg

More Myrtle Avenue

Our driveway at the house on Myrtle Avenue consisted of two long strips of cement. They started at the street and went all the way up to the one car garage. (I think it's called a ribbon driveway.) If my parents didn't place the car wheels perfectly on the cement platforms, the car would slide off the track and tear up the grass between them. Perfect for our bikes, wagons, and whatever other things had wheels on it, including my sister Carol's baby buggy.

We played a game where I was the traffic cop and Sue and John drove their vehicles up and down the "highway." I started and stopped them for imaginary red and green lights. I used an intuitive built-in timer to determine how long they should stop for a red light. Simple play, yes, but play that kept us enthralled for long summer hours.

This driveway was also great for hopscotch. We would chalk it up with squares and numbers. That provided more hours of fun. Come to think of it, we drew all kinds of things on that driveway. Mom and Dad didn't care because the rain would eventually take all of the art away—good and bad—and then we'd start all over again.

We were kids. There were a lot of skinned up knees at our house. To this day, I still have a scar on my knee from learning how to ride a two-wheeler on that driveway. Turns out, I wasn't ready to "let go." And, when I finally did, I crashed into one of our basement window wells along the side of the house. I guess I just didn't have the whole balance thing down yet.

In the early 1960's, we watched black and white TV. We had one TV upstairs in our little family room and another little one in the basement. That one was kind of fuzzy, but Dad used to watch boxing on that set. Then the day arrived when Dad decided that it was time for a color television. Holy moly! That was big! I remember the big TV box entering the house. We kids loved that box and turned it into a play-thing, like a big doll house.

To unveil the "living color," we invited my dad's folks over, Hanna and William Nyberg. Their favorite show at the time was *The Lawrence Welk Show* and, their drink of choice was the highball, (a combination of whiskey and 7 UP). So, of course, highballs were served to mark this special occasion. I'll never forget seeing the NBC peacock fanning out all those colored tail feathers. NBC would be wise to bring back this kind of nostalgic charm. Do you remember the three chimes that accompanied the peacock? I do.

Did moments such as this one seed my career in television? That big box, the color TV, the celebration with family.... Such little things can chart the course of a life.

*   *   *

This seems like a good time to introduce you to my dad's parents. Hanna and William were immigrants from Sweden. They worked hard to support my dad and his sister, Adele. Grandma Nyberg drove only once in her entire life, and it was to take a friend to get some tomatoes. Picture a Lucy-Ethel-type adventure. You know, like that duo of adventurous, albeit naïve, ladies on the *I Love Lucy* TV show. Gram didn't have a driver's license, but they went anyway. They were just going to get tomatoes after all, and they did. They got their stash and made it home, but then (yes, there is a "but then") but then, the garage got in the way when she tried to stop the car. She drove it through the closed garage door. They weren't hurt, but that was the last time she ever drove. I can assure you. It's too bad, really. In those days being a "stay at home" wife or mother could be very isolating.

Hanna was a very accomplished baker. Desserts and breads were her thing. People cherished her delectable delights. She baked for everyone—her church congregation, friends, strangers—anyone. This talent helped her find community as an immigrant. Her English was not very good, and she was shy. The baked goods were her introduction to people. They produced friendships.

Immigrants often faced challenging times when they arrived in America. This was true for my grandparents. They worked hard and made-do. They struggled and eventually prospered into middle class. Even though they didn't have much money, my grandmother would always go out of her way for people my grandfather would bring home, feeding them her homemade soups, breads and desserts. For her, food was love. As is true in so many cultures.

One of my dads' friends from high school went on to become an Oscar-winning movie director and actor. Sydney Irwin Pollack, was prolific; he directed dozens of films and television shows. Pollack won an Academy Award for the 1985 film *Out of Africa*. Pollack's parents were Jewish immigrants from Ukraine who divorced when he was very young. There were troubles in his home. So, from time to time, Syd would seek some peace in my dad's home. He would have meals there. Pollack moved away from South Bend to get on with what would become his very famous life. Dad got on with his life in South Bend. They didn't keep in touch, but Mom and Dad, and everybody else who knew him from South Bend watched from afar as Pollack's career thrived. They were proud of him.

For some reason my parents made it a point to never intrude in people's lives—ever—they pretty much kept to themselves and were happy for others. I wonder if this thinking was to their detriment in some ways. They could have had a lot more fun with friends, but chose to keep a distance. I did not adopt this way of thinking. During my teenage years, I'd throw parties for friends and relatives whenever I could. I did all of the organizing, including inviting lots of people to our house.

As a young adult, my brother did seek out Pollack while on a trip to Los Angeles. Pollack, to his credit, made room for him in his very busy schedule. John told me he couldn't have been any warmer to him. He talked to John about his times in South Bend and reminisced about growing up with our dad. Pollack never forgot where he came from and stayed in touch with many in South Bend over the years. He also helped the community support the performing arts by making donations and such. Sometimes, he would return for class reunions. I think those moments Pollack spent with my brother, John, brought back fond memories, including the time he spent in Grammy Nyberg's tiny little kitchen. My brother was sure to say, "Hi" for my dad. Pollack was happy about that.

When Pollack died in 2008, my parents were very sad.

Home is where you are nourished.
—Ann Nyberg

What's in a Name?

Every family renames stuff, right? Oh boy, were we good at that. For instance, "mashed beseptents," what does that mean? Time's up... "mashed potatoes" of course.

Each one of us had nicknames that we gave each other. Some of them kind of made sense, while others made no sense at all. Ann Louise was "Ant," "Column Legs," or "No-ankle, Annie." Sue was "Sister" or "Swellen" because her middle name is Ellen. Yep, after, Mom. John William was "Goat," "June," "Joan," or "Mooger." Carol Hope was called "Gobdid" and "Narolina Jones." I could go into a lot of detail about these names, but I won't. You get the idea. We were a little nuts.

My brother shared a room with our baby sister, Carol. Sue and I shared a room that had twin beds. They were close enough together that we could jump back and forth from one bed to the next. When it was time to go to bed, we'd take a running leap from outside the bedroom and jump onto our beds. We did this because we thought something or someone might be under the beds and grab our ankles. Did you ever do that as a kid?

One day, Sue and I got so upset with each other that we dumped the contents of each other's desks all over the floor. What a mess. We both started to cry. We hugged each other and apologized. (We were 18 months apart, living in close quarters so sometimes we got on each other's nerves.) So silly, really. We couldn't love each other any more than we do, but sometimes sisters just do things like that.

John was the type of baby that did a lot of head-banging in his crib. He bucked back and forth. Stubborn. I think that's how he got the nickname "Goat." Goats buck and ram into things. Interesting how he grew up to be such a mild-mannered adult. Go figure.

Then, there was the crayon episode. John took a crayon and wrote "boys" on the wall in his room. I guess he was tired of being around sisters and was declaring his independence. Of course, I decided those letters should stand for something, an acronym. So I said to my sister, Sue, "BOYS" will stand for "Beast of Yogurt Shells." Leaves you shaking your head doesn't it? Where did that come from and what exactly does that mean? Sue thought that was just great and we went with it. Sue and I thought John might be putting together some kind of boy's club and we wanted to make sure we knew all about it. One never materialized.

Three girls and one boy, I really should sit down and talk to John about what that was like for him. I'm sure he felt like we were ganging up on him half the time. Maybe we were. We were three strong-willed girls.

Because my dad was in private practice, we watched him work hard setting up his office. He would take us there on weekends. He had two rooms set up in which to see patients. So naturally, that's what we did as well. Our bedrooms became dental exam rooms and even had a secretarial area, just like his. Sue liked being the secretary.

Mom would be ironing downstairs and we would be upstairs conducting a dental practice. We took turns being the patient and the dentist. We filled out a day's schedule as we booked all our fictitious patients.

Our Mom played bridge and would, occasionally, host the card party at our house. Seven lady friends would come over on a weeknight, leaving their husbands at home to watch the kids. Two card tables would go up in the living room. This meant fun doings for us kids. There would, undoubtedly, be some fancy food around. That was the only time we had something called "bridge mix," a variety of chocolates put into a pretty candy bowl. There would be other sweet treats too, including Thin Mints from Fanny May. They were rectangular-shaped and very, very thin. A layer of chocolate coated the outside and there was a thin green layer of mint in the middle. Back then, you could peel the layers apart. That was fun. Mom would have my other favorites too: white chocolate with pieces of peppermint candy inside. Enacting our own sting operation, we would sneak a little bit of the candy prior to the ladies' arrival. One at a time, we'd slither around and take a single piece out of the bowl. Sue and I would take turns telling each other when the coast was clear.

Our Mom never wasted money on too many goodies. That candy and bridge mix was special. If there were any leftovers, we gobbled them up the next day.

Having people over was a big deal; the house was freshened and cleaned. On the rare occasion that the four of us kids are together now as adults, the host location is spotless within moments of someone saying, "Hey let's have a party."

My siblings and I are all parents now. We have nine children in total. Sadly, we are far-flung across the United States, but remain very close. The times we shared on Myrtle Avenue have kept us tight.

If you're lucky enough to be loved by your siblings,
you're blessed. The bond is forever.
—Ann Nyberg

Chaos at Birch Lake

W hat is it about being or living near the water that is so soothing? As humans we are drawn to oceans, lakes, ponds and streams. If one doesn't exist we create them and put houses around them. I would never want to be very far from a beach. Worst case scenario, I would make certain to vacation near water.

I grew up not too far from Lake Michigan; it was our "ocean." That was the largest body of water I saw in my childhood. The state of Michigan is full of lakes, big and small. In 1964, my mother's dad and mom, Chester and Ann, bought a 900 square foot cottage on Birch Lake, a 300 acre spring-fed body of water. The water is clear and very deep, 90 feet down in some spots.

The cottage is a one-story-no-frills-gem of a place. It is made of knotty pine, has two small bedrooms, a tiny bathroom, and a spacious kitchen-living room area where over the years—more than 50 years—we have all come together.

The cottage, dubbed "Chaos" by my grandparents, and rightfully so, has seen five generations of us now passing through it. There have been birthday parties, card playing, pot luck dinners—you name it, it's happened there. My aunt Martha and uncle Gordon lived there for several months while they were building a home. I even think somebody might have spent a honeymoon there. It's a little slice of heaven.

The cottage came with a giant TV antenna. In those days, you had to have this monstrous contraption in order to get any reception at all. This was especially true at the cottage; the trees towered over that little dwelling. I remember thinking that the antenna seemed to reach as high as the sky. We had to rotate it from inside to try and get the best reception. It was a riot to see that erecter-set-style tower revolving. It took some direct hits from lightning during thunderstorms until it was eventually taken down.

We watched the Miss America pageant every September. We crowded around the "tube," trying to make out the faces of the contestants amid the snowy reception. In her youth, my aunt Martha had been a runner-up in the Miss Indiana pageant. We were a patriotic family and the Miss America pageant used to stand for the red-white-and-blue-Mom's-apple-pie kind of patriotism. So, you watched it and hoped the home state gal would win.

Aunt Martha had a daughter named Margaret. Sue and I and Margaret are all close in age and we hung out a lot together as teenagers. One year, on the weekend of the Miss America pageant, we used the pier in front of the cottage as a runway and pretended to be contestants, perfecting our walks in our bathing suits. Imagine what the neighbors were thinking, watching this! We could not have cared less. We were serious about getting the walk and the spins just right.

The pier was made of wood planks. It was heavy to put in and take out. That was work for the menfolk. In 1976, we painted the planks red, white and blue to coincide with the 200th year of the founding of our country. I'm sure that was my idea, and I talked the family into it. My grandparents were so happy that the whole extended family spent a lot of time at the cottage; they were delighted to see us all making memories. I am so glad that I have these stories to tell.

After my grandparents passed, Mom and her sister, Martha, and brother, Montie, inherited the cottage. It was built in the 1940's and only small changes have been made since then. You can clean it in two seconds, and that's how the family wants to keep it.

The very cool looking 1940's electric stove that came with the cottage was replaced in the summer of 2014. It had become a fire hazard, so the family agreed that it had to go. We managed to get a more modern "icebox," what we called a refrigerator, a few years back. It's arrival resulted in a ban on fishing worms in the kitchen; they were relegated to a little fridge out in the garage. The lamps in the place are also mostly original, but have been rewired. Everything is very simple. That's why it works.

The exterior of the cottage was originally white. We repainted it white for years, until somebody said, "Enough with the white!" Pale yellow was voted on as the new color. A few members of the family didn't like the yellow at first because it was different, but the color has grown on them, I think. A front screen porch was added too. That was a pretty smart idea. The porch keeps the mosquitoes away, while providing a landing platform for the thousands and thousands of Mayflies that come calling during the summer. I swear, you can watch them grow right on the screen. Yuck! Their life span is only about a day, but they just keep coming. What a chore it is to sweep their little bodies off the screens.

There is a lot of naugahyde in the cottage. It is perfect for kids with wet bathing suits. As you will recall, I have faith in naugahyde.

The dishes in the cottage are all mismatched. We do have full sets of silverware. So many forks and spoons went missing that we had to replenish them (you have to have utensils for potluck suppers) but we are lacking bowls. If you want popcorn, it might be served to you in a big plastic strainer that somebody got at a dollar store. That's all just fine. Who cares?

The cottage is situated in a lagoon area of the lake. If you're a golfer, think of it as a dog leg left. Across from our cottage, in the cove, is Camp Tanadoonah. The camp is at least 100 years old. It's a sleepover camp for boys and girls. Many of us have gone to the camp, some were counselors too. Most members of the family loved it, but not me. I can wax poetic about it now, but I just wasn't a happy camper. I was supposed to be a camper there while in third grade. Right after my folks dropped me off at the camp, I started explaining to the hierarchy why I needed to leave and go stay at my cottage across the cove with my parents. I was homesick, and there were bugs and dry peanut butter sandwiches and cold oatmeal. I'm sure that it was nowhere near as bad as I'm making it sound, but it just wasn't for me. I hated camping and thus never sent my three daughters to camp.

I went back to Camp Tanadoonah for the first time in 2013 for a fundraiser. I have to say, it's a pretty cool place, if you like to camp. When it's "lights out" time at the camp, a recording of "Taps" is played. Then things get very quiet. As an adult, I love watching the kids at the camp but that's as close to camping as I need to be.

When I was a kid, I cut my journalistic teeth at Birch Lake. I wrote stories for the only publication, the *Birch Barker*. It still exists today. In the summer of 2014, I rifled through the weekly publication to see what was going on in the area. I started thinking to myself, if I lived here all summer, I would write for it again. This time around I would come to the *Barker* with nearly four decades worth of television news experience. I know how to uncover all kinds of things. A gossip column might be fun. Maybe, someday.

The lake cottage is a pretty special place. For a lot of years I didn't get to enjoy it. I was too busy working in Oklahoma and Connecticut, and raising kids. I am now getting to enjoy it again. I am making sure my grown kids—no matter where they settle—get back there for a week or two in the summer. They need to understand what life is all about at the lake.

Life at the lake, nothing like it.
—Ann Nyberg

Coffee, Java, Joe

When I was little, my grammy Waggoner used to have tea parties for us. Her real first name was Anna. Anna Devries, no middle name. I was her namesake. I am "Ann" because she didn't like the name "Anna." Her friends all called her, Ann. I was called, Annie.

Grammy was a twin. I am her namesake and I have twins. Because Sue, Cousin Margaret and I all lived in South Bend, we were able to attend quite a few of Grammy's little tea parties. She would give us watered-down coffee loaded with milk and sugar in fancy china cups. She had a collection of them. So many that we could select a different cup for each party. We felt grown-up. We pretended that we were ladies enjoying a cup of coffee out on the town. Grammy was one of eleven children. Her parents were Dutch. Maybe her Mom did tea parties with her, we're not sure. Sue, Margaret and I would sit at a little table and chat with her. These were cherished moments.

Fast forward. In high school—I think my junior year—I picked up coffee drinking in earnest. I routinely met girlfriends for coffee to talk about this or that. In college, at Purdue University in West Lafayette, Indiana, caffeine became a necessity for late night study sessions, cramming for exams, trying to get that paper done for the next day.

Out of college, with a degree in journalism, I hit the streets as a TV reporter in Elkhart, Indiana. My shift started at 5 a.m. so that meant getting up at 3:30 a.m. to get to work on time. Caffeine to the rescue. I drove a yellow 1972 automatic stick shift Volkswagen Beetle with a sun roof. With coffee in my hand, off to work I would go, signing on the TV station bright and early.

Just as a side note for anyone who doesn't know the inner-workings of the Volkswagen "bug." The heaters in them were atrocious, nearly non-existent. The engine is in the back and the trunk is in the front. When you turned the heat on in my car, the interior smelled of gasoline. It was terrible on icy roads. This was a car that should have only been driven in the summer. Then, it was great fun.

I called the car "Louise." That's my middle name. I ended up giving Louise to my brother after I bought another car. Louise then headed south; she ported my brother back and forth from South Bend to Middle Tennessee State University. That is until the day she died in Munfordville, Kentucky (and there is actually some bizarre irony to her having ended in that specific town). Yes, another good story.

The yellow bug is dead down there in Kentucky, out in the boondocks. My twenty-year-old brother manages to get it to a filling station. My parents drive down and pick him up. They tell the mechanic at the filling station they'll be back for the car. "Just fix it." Well, Mom thinks this guy got frustrated with Louise because he couldn't fix her. He ended up torching her! Yep, dear Louise was set on fire. My brother saw some of her remains in a charred heap.

Now here is where it gets really interesting. Louise met her demise in the very same middle-of-nowhere place that our relative, John Waggoner, was taken prisoner in the Civil War. He was 17 or 18. This is where "The Siege of Munfordville" occurred. It was a turning point in the war. Munfordville had a railroad bridge over the Green River, a key station on the Louisville & Nashville Railroad. Confederate control of this vital transportation hub greatly affected the Union movements for the rest of the War. Do ghosts destroy cars?

The morale of this little story: Stay out of Munfordville!

*   *   *

Back to coffee. Caffeine has fueled my near 40 year career in journalism, taking me from Elkhart, to Oklahoma City, to Connecticut and points in-between.

I learned to mainline caffeine in the early years. When you work on deadline and at odd hours, you have to be on your game. A steamy mug of "joe" does it for me, every time.

What is my favorite coffee? I'm a Dunkin' Donuts gal. I learned to love this brand after I came to Connecticut. I would order a small D&D coffee with cream at the drive-thru as my photographer and I headed out to a story. We used to know every D&D across the state.

I got really good at holding coffee in the car while we raced to a story. I developed shocks in my wrist, just like on a car; bumps were no problem. I could maneuver a cup of joe without a lid and not spill a drop. I often worked with a veteran photographer in the field, Pat Child. He has since passed. There are not many people like him in the business today. He was a real newsman through and through. Pat could do the same thing with his coffee in the car; he mastered the technique long before I did. Together, we covered a ton of stories in Connecticut: KKK stakeouts, murders, the L'Ambiance building collapse in Bridgeport and the tornado that hit Bantam in 1989.

In the 1980's, Pat and I worked very well with first responders. When you're covering breaking stories in the field, you develop relationships with police officers and firefighters. Many times, we ended up sharing a coffee with them, waiting for events to develop on the scene.

I remember being on the U.S. Coast Guard cutter, *Ballard*, on what felt like the coldest day ever in Connecticut. We were out on the deck as the crew worked its way up and down the Connecticut River, breaking up the ice so boats could pass. When I got below, the crew had a cup of hot steaming coffee waiting for me. What a gift!

In a diner, the best cup of coffee is served in a real honest-to-goodness vintage dinnerware mug, the kind that's really heavy and scratched up a bit. That's what we called "seasoned." On a cold winter's day, that cup warms your hands. If you put your face over it, the steam gives you a mini facial. To say that I love coffee is a bit of an understatement.

The Northeast and in particular Connecticut, has a lot of wonderful diners, many of them are vintage. A diner is my favorite place to meet someone, to have a conversation. You can get whatever you want there, even a glass of wine. A diner with old time dinnerware gets an A+ in my book. Give me a "Blue Plate Special" anytime.

Diners are great equalizers. No matter how rich or how poor you are, you can eat in a diner. It's affordable and you never know who you might be sitting next to on one of those swivel seats at the bar, or in the next booth over. Diners go way back in U.S. history. Initially, they were a place for a cheap meal when times were tough. Most were small, modest spaces. People crammed inside, sitting close together. They served a purpose then, just as they do today. Diners can be a place for people to come together and be equals under one roof.

A cup of coffee in a diner is a little slice of heaven.
—Ann Nyberg

Nooked in a Booth

*I*f you're going to eat in a diner, you should ask for a booth, period. Sliding way back into a corner is perfect; you feel "hugged." How is it that time just passes as you converse and eat in these little spaces? I do tend to "settle" in and eventually have no idea what time it is. The turnover of booths in diners can't be that good, at least, not when I'm there. I've been known to wait for a booth if one is not available. My sisters and brother will do that too.

It's all good in a diner—the naugahyde seats, the formica tables, the swivel bar stools. Diner life is comprised of a little community that changes hour by hour. It's a kind of living room where many conversations are going on at the same time. Look around you the next time you're in a diner, you'll see a lot of slices of life. There are business deals being discussed as well as serious and light-hearted chats between people. You might see a baseball team come in after practice or maybe a game. Diners represent generations of lives, both the young and the old.

In northern Indiana there were sandwich shops and lunch places, but not too many real honest-to-goodness diners. We didn't have the luxury of seeing neon signs out in front of an eatery with shiny steel facades. Thankfully, the Northeast has afforded me that treat.

What about the waiters and waitresses in diners? Some stay for decades. I can't help but ask myself what makes them tick? Do they like what they do? I sat down with a waitress I had seen for years at a place along the shoreline of Connecticut to ask her why she does what she does.

It turns out that she (we'll call her "Susan") has been waiting tables for nearly her whole adult life, with the exception of a few years when she was at home raising her two young sons. She started waitressing in 1973 and was still at it in 2014. She told me when she started waiting tables, during the deregulation of trucking in Connecticut, she was at a place in the town of Orange. There were at least five diners there at the time. Orange had trucking terminals and she would get to know all the guys who made their living on the road. They would come in many times a week for a meal, sometimes twice a day.

Susan met her first husband in a diner. She met the second one in a restaurant. Her whole life is pretty much about diners and about the lives of the people who frequent them. She loves the life of "serving it up." She has seen families grow over the years. Babies have been born and customers have died. Diner clients and staff are extended family members to her.

Susan told me a story about what keeps her coming back to the diner. First of all, she genuinely cares about people, and her customers care about her. One day, she got word that an elderly woman, whom she had waited on for years, lost her husband. She felt sad and wasn't sure what she should do. She didn't know the woman all that well but her heart felt as if she did. She asked a lot of questions of people at the diner and figured out where the widow lived. She baked her a chocolate cake and brought it over to her house. She wasn't sure how the woman would receive her gift, but that didn't matter. She just had to show her she cared. To her delight, the woman was thrilled. She told her she was touched that someone would work so hard to find her and to reach out in that way. It was a small simple thing—baking a cake—but it represented something much larger: Humans caring about each other.

Every dollar counts with Susan. She goes to work every day with empty pockets and comes home with tips that people care to pay her, dollars add up. If even one dollar is missing or she gets stiffed, it matters, it matters a lot. The work is hard and sometimes people don't appreciate her. Some treat her like nothing more than hired help and are rude and uncaring. She can spot those kinds of people a mile away. If she can, she avoids them. She doesn't want to endure the unpleasant experience. She loves what she does on most days and doesn't want to be "invisible" to people she waits on. She truly wants to know how your day is going.

Susan loved the hit television show *Alice* that ran from 1976 through 1985. *Alice* was about a widow who moved to Arizona with her son and found work at a roadside diner called, "Mel's." Susan relates to that show. When she was very young and wore waitress dresses, the tips were bigger from the guys, not that she flirted or anything. It was just a fact. When she wore slacks, the tips were less. So she wore more dresses. Her pockets would be fuller at the end of the day. She considered it just part of the job, to help make ends meet.

Susan still loves what she does. Her philosophy is simple. She asks, "Where else can you work in a place where you can talk all day and get fed and be surrounded by people who are more than strangers?" This is the life in which she flourishes.

Susan had to have a double knee replacement and was home for three months. She missed her job so much she couldn't wait to get back on her feet. She wanted to find out what had been going on in their lives while she was away.

Susan knows how well the economy is doing, not by the size of the tips, but the amount of times people do or don't come into the diner. They stay away altogether when times are tough.

Patrons over the years have gotten to know her and have shown they care about her. A few years back, one of her grown sons got into a very bad motorcycle accident and had to have surgery. It happened right around Christmas time. While caring for him, she couldn't make the hundreds of cookies that she made every year for folks. She didn't have the time or the energy. A customer felt sad about this and asked her, "If you could have cookies around the house, what kind would they be?" Susan said, "Mexican Tea Cake cookies." You know where this is going next. Right? That's exactly what she got. Mexican Tea Cake cookies were dropped off at her home. She was so happy.

Susan says that no one goes out to eat more than waitresses, especially her crowd. When they aren't serving up the food, they're out eating it. She and her waitress friends are "foodies." Funny thing about Susan, growing up her family never, ever, went out to eat. She said her dad was too particular about his food. Still, every once and a while, he would stop and buy good bread and bring it home.

Despite the fact that there is no pension, no big bonuses, nothing at the end of a waitress' career, Susan says that she wouldn't trade what she does for the world. She loves every minute of it. She has had a chance to live vicariously through her customers' lives, which has in turn enriched her life.

I am so happy to have gotten to know, Susan. I get to tell a little of her story so that anybody reading about her might understand what goes on in the mind of that person that is serving you in a diner. At the end of the interview she remarked, "See you at the diner." That made me smile. It still does.

Never go on a second date with a man
who was rude to a waitress.
—Susan

This is Not a Dress Rehearsal

The older I get and the more life I observe, the more I know how important it is to live in the moment. It is important to tell people you love them, to try and make your corner of the world a better place.

I run into people all the time who say, "One day I'm going to do this or that." I just tell them straight out, "Don't wait. Do it now!" You get one life. This isn't a dress rehearsal for a play at a later date. As much as I tell this to people, I am constantly reminding myself about this too. Yes, life is short, and there are no guarantees about what lies ahead. You can make all the plans in the world, but things happen—good and bad things—that throw all of those plans off course. Much of this is completely out of our control. None of us likes that. We would like to think we can stick to whatever plan we've made, but truly there are so many outside forces. In the end, it's going to be what it's going to be.

I am "type A," so I get bored easily and am always onto something new. This is both good and bad. If you're so busy heading toward the next adventure, you sometimes miss the one you're in, you forget to enjoy it. It's over and you can't get that time back.

That's another thing about life, time is precious. You hear that all of the time, but still we waste countless hours doing things we shouldn't or spend time with people that suck the life out of us. We need to get our priorities straight and get rid of the nonsense, but sometimes that's tough to do. If you have friends who are no longer feeding your soul or won't be around when times are tough, rethink the time you spend with them. Because women are sentimental beings and nurturers, it's more difficult for us to leave friendships behind. We don't want to hurt feelings, but if you're not having fun, you're wasting time and your life.

When a family member or friend dies or someone you love faces a life-threatening illness, you realize in that moment that things just happen. It makes you realize that you too may be running out of time on the planet.

Here's another saying you hear all the time, "Stop and smell the roses." Okay, so you do that and then what? You just move on. Sayings like that have been around for generations for a reason, because it's true. Take stock of your life, sit down, watch people, think of how you might be a little better to others the next day. Think about your family and their needs and not your own. And, yes, stop and smell the roses and, maybe, buy them for someone as an unexpected gift.

We live in a world that is moving so fast, too fast. What are you doing with the hours in your day? The workday is no longer defined. Because of cell phones and electronic devices, you can be contacted by your boss at any time of the day or night. And, guess what? When you read or listen to a message, that means you're working, you're on the clock. You may not have to act on the task right that minute, but you're thinking about it. You've just given away your precious time.

You need to be around people who help you be at your best and understand when you need help. How many relationships do you see that on the surface are not healthy? These only result in more wasted time.

My husband and I raised three daughters. Hopefully, we instilled in them a sense of who they are, one that is solid enough not to be manipulated by other's perceptions of who they should be. I want them to be with partners who bring out the best in them.

Respect is a big issue in our household, especially respect of others. I don't see a ton of that around anymore. With social media platforms comes those "comments." Many rude people hide, often anonymously, behind those comments. Hurtful things are written. What kind of a world is this? A lot of harm can come from this, especially to the vulnerable. This has led to cyber bullying.

Civility is disappearing. When was the last time you heard "please" and "thank you" or "excuse me"? How many times has a door been slammed in your face as you're trying to enter a building? Nobody is paying attention to the people around them.

This all-about-me attitude is a huge problem. It's not all about you. It's about all of us. The work ethic seen post World War II is nearly non-existent in many places. What happened to the "work hard, play hard" mentality?

Everybody is looking down at their cell phones, even running into walls because they can't take their eyes off of information coming at them. Jeez, get off the phone and see what is going on around you. We have to figure out how to keep people from living in their computers and cell phones. It's great for connecting, but it is now our ball and chain. They keep us from having real conversations with others, real relationships. The art of conversation is fading away; people just text, they don't call anymore. I can't remember the last time my phone rang in the newsroom. That's just crazy.

Are acts of kindness now just random? You have no idea what is going on in the lives of people you meet, no idea. Jumping to conclusions is very dangerous. Words can hurt—spoken or written—and we have to pay more attention to that. Think about the big picture before you speak. Once words are spoken, they're out there and you can't take them back. You can apologize all you want and maybe the apology will be accepted but, still, that's a moment in time you can't pull back.

When I first got into television news, I had a consultant tell me (and wisely so), "You are writing about someone's husband, child, wife, friend. It's personal, remember that. Stick to the who, what, when, where, why, and how of stories and as a reporter you will be doing your job."

Before you hit send, think carefully
about how your words might be perceived.
—Ann Nyberg

Sunday Dinner

I'm a knitter. My maternal grammy, Ann, taught me how to put two sticks together and come up with some kind of garment. She's the one who threw all the tea parties for us kids, I told you about earlier.

Ann was one of eleven children. Her parents immigrated to America from Friesland, in the northern part of the Netherlands. Ann's parents were "teetotalers," they didn't drink alcoholic beverages, nor did they work on the Sabbath. They were Dutch Reform.

My mom's dad, Chester, was an only child. Talk about different family backgrounds. My grandmother shared everything she had and helped to raise all of her brothers and sisters. My grandpa Chet never had to share anything.

His mom, Cordelia (or Cordie), used to have Sunday dinners for the extended family at her house. The dinner was actually in the mid-afternoon so that the hearty meal could keep you full for the day. Green beans with bacon and potatoes were Sunday dinner staples. My mom continued that tradition into my childhood. I have made this dish for my family too. All of the ingredients go into one pot on the stove.

This was good planning; family gathering around a big table, chatting about the week they just had and the week to come, great food that didn't cost a bundle, very practical. When was the last time you did that with your family, sat around a dinner table and really talked about things? We're all moving so fast. Who has time for that? Well, we should make time. The lack of events like this contributes to communication problems in families. In the end, we're not talking to each other.

As a kid, and even as an adult, I always tried stretching the heck out of Sunday. Having a get-together made the day fun and got rid of that "Sunday feeling." Did you ever have that? That's what my family called it; it's a type of dread that the weekend was ending.

When I was in high school, I would stand over the counter shoving dinner down my throat. There was so much going on, I didn't think that I had time to sit down and eat. My kids did that too. Going, going, going. It's just the way things are. This is a crazy way to live.

However, as my kids were growing up they got to know the thrill of Sunday dinners. Thanks go to my southern friend, Missy, who was raised for much of her life in Vicksburg, Mississippi. Missy put on so many family Sunday dinners at her house, it was a virtual Disneyland in her backyard. There were all kinds of goings-on there, games, food, conversation. My family was always invited as was another good friend, Tina and her crew, she had five daughters. All the kids loved it. It was like a mini holiday when we came together. It was potluck style—everyone brought a dish. It was a grand way to start a new week.

When immigrant families first came to the U.S., three-family homes sprung up so they could live more affordably. While that might be a little too close for some, it meant family was there when you needed them.

When the economy went sour in the U.S. in 2008, it forced families to pare down and come back together. With college costs sky-high and not enough jobs for graduates, that has kids moving back home. Maybe, in the long run, this isn't all together a terrible thing.

Debt is eating the country alive and it's forcing us to rethink everything. We have a disappearing middle class which, of course, is what our country was built on, hard-working folks who were proud of everything they owned. Excess has gotten the best of us. How much stuff do you really need?

In Indiana, when we were little, we did the potluck suppers a lot. Everybody brought something so that no one had to carry the whole responsibility or cost of putting up a meal.

We can learn a lot from the past. We need to talk to our elders and learn things from them. I believe you have to go back to the past to find the future.

If we don't do this, we'll keep making the same mistakes. That's why history is so important. Go out and read about it and understand it.

Somebody who has lived a long time knows things—a lot of things—and they can impart that information to you if you just ask. I think the older you get the more invisible you get. Our society loves youth, but seniors should be revered and respected. They've had a long journey and in that journey things can be learned that current generations don't know. Don't wait till it's too late. Talk to your elders and see what they know.

Go back to the past to find your future.
—Ann Nyberg

Civility, Where is It?

If you want to take a look at a slice of society, go to the mall. Take a look at what is going on there. Go on a mission to see how people are really acting. People watch. Take it all in. A lot of people are in their own worlds, completely unaware of anybody else.

When I was growing up, I was taught to look people in the eye and acknowledge them; it means "Hi, how are you?" or "Have a nice day". It's a pleasantry. Because everybody is moving so fast these days and looking down at mobile devices, they don't have a clue what is going on around them.

For grins, I did this one day just to see what is going on in society. Try it yourself. Make it a point to hold doors for everyone coming in and going out of stores, or let someone go ahead of you in line at the counter. Buy a cup of coffee for the next person in line. See how they react. Odds are they'll be shocked that someone would be so kind. Do they even notice random acts of kindness? If they are thrilled that someone would care enough to be so kind, they might just pass on the goodwill through a selfless act of their own.

I'm not even sure if younger generations recognize a kinder gentler world. This is troubling to me. I wonder what my grandchildren will find when they arrive on this planet. People tell me all the time that they don't like how they're being treated, but what are they doing to change their situation? Most just give up and think, "Well, that's just the way it is". Where are the civility police to keep people in check? There needs to be a squadron of game-changers around to catch people off-guard with random acts of kindness and see if it catches on.

Don't get me wrong, there are many, many kind souls

on this planet, doing wonderful things for others. That said, the world in which we find ourselves today just feels different than when I was a kid. People are not caring enough about each other.

Rudeness extends to driving too. I'm certain you've been cut off on the road or nearly been hit by someone texting and driving. We're a gotta-get-there-faster-and-stay-in-touch-24/7 world. When I was a young driver, I felt so guilty if I wasn't driving according to laws. We actually did stop at red lights instead of gunning it though red because people "gotta get there." Were standards higher in the past?

I feel strongly that things are headed in the wrong direction. People don't want to have conversations anymore either. They find them too time consuming. Can you imagine this? Nobody has time to stop and talk? I know when someone is just "phoning in" a conversation with me, don't you? That's an indication they don't have time to listen. I can see the thought bubble above their head and it says, "Yeah, whatever." Because we are not listening, we are not learning from each other.

Don't you wish you could fast forward about 50 years into the future and find out how society is going to end up? Right now, that thought is a bit frightening.

If it's all about you, good luck when you need assistance.
The helpers will have all moved on.
—Ann Nyberg

Dear Diary...

The written word is everything to me. It's no wonder I grew up to tell stories for a living. Name a topic, I'm all in. I'm fascinated to get "under the hood" and find out some part of a story that no one knows about and tell others.

The passion for writing probably started in 1966, the year I got a five-year diary for Christmas from my mom. I still have that diary. It has a lock on the front. I can't find the key now, but when I was little, after I wrote my entries, I locked it and hid it under my bed or in a drawer where no one could find it. I wrote in pencil just in case I had to erase something. Day after day, I jotted down kid-like things that I thought about. In the beginning, it

79

was a lot of after school events, like doctor's appointments and meetings and people coming over to my house. I stuffed things into it too, like napkins from restaurants, movie and concert tickets, and slumber party invites. I had the need to collect things that were a part of my life, to document my life. I was a sentimental kid who grew up to be a sentimental adult. My diary got so fat that I couldn't lock it anymore. I had to make sure to hide it well from my siblings.

I love knowing what I was thinking about back then on a particular date. As I have moved on in years, dates get more and more meaningful. My grandpa Waggoner always put a date on everything. Every card he ever got had a date put on it immediately and that turned out to be a lovely gift. When we went through his things, after he passed in his early 90's, it helped us remember exactly when events happened and stories then came to mind.

History is important, family history is everything when it comes to the generations coming up behind. Maybe my little diary will mean something to my kids and grandkids someday. I cherished it as a child. I put all my thoughts in it. My oldest daughter, Lindsay, took a look at it for the first time when she was 28. She got such a kick out of what her mom was thinking at age eight. I loved watching her read it and hold it in her hands. It took me back some fifty years, to when I was a little girl holding it in my hands. Those oh-so-very-innocent years! It was a special mother-daughter moment.

When my three daughters were young, I started diaries for them and we shared them. They would write their thoughts to me and I would answer back. Each daughter individually holds secrets with me. So many words over the years. We confided in each other about the trials and tribulations of growing up. Their diaries were a safe space for each one of them. We worked through a lot of things in those years with words and those volumes are cherished. I have them in a special drawer and from time to time I go back and read what they wrote to me and me to them, raw thoughts about what mattered. So many beautiful passages. Those writing times between the four of us are gone now, but the words will forever remain in their handwriting, in print and cursive. (Who knew that cursive writing would nearly cease to exist in such a short time after we did this?) They will have their words and mine—a representation of our time together—long after I have left the planet.

I would recommend that moms and dads do this with their children—to create a record of their lives together. Even if you can't write every day, the journal is there for your children to write down their thoughts. It's a way to talk with each other, to keep communication going when they (or you) can't find the words to speak. You'll be surprised at how many problems can be worked out this way.

You only pass through once,
memories will fade but words are forever.
—Ann Nyberg

The Little Black Skirt

You ou really don't need a closet full of clothes to look your best as a woman. If you take a look at the "dress code" for females in Europe, you'll find that if you have just a few good pieces of clothing and good shoes, you're good to go. To make it look like you have a ton of outfits, the trick is to have a multitude of scarves and some jewelry (we're talking costume jewelry) and you're all set.

Never mind the little black dress, a little black skirt can go a long way. I know this because I exercise this technique. As long as you switch up your top, no one has a clue that you're wearing the same black skirt. Talk about cost-effective!

People hardly ever look down, they look at your face. I bet if you asked someone in your workplace what you wore the day before they couldn't tell you. Women in the U.S. are so obsessed with having more and more and more. They don't realize that less is more.

Try this out the next time you travel somewhere. These days the airlines will barely let you take a suitcase the size of a purse, so you have to pare down anyway. Lay out your outfits on the bed before you take off and you'll see what I mean. You can make it appear as if you have taken a steamer trunk full of clothes with you on your vacation.

The scarf is a miracle worker when it comes to looking like you have a ton of outfits. You can tie it in a million different ways. To me it's like a necklace and you can wear them year round—really light ones for summer and big bulky ones for winter.

When I was growing up, nobody had walk-in closets. Closets were small. You might have had just a wardrobe or a dresser. Women lived their whole lives without 50 different dresses or 50 pairs of shoes. This whole notion of excess is out of control.

Women in New York City have known about a trick too, for years. Black skirts, tights, and flats. It looks sophisticated and you can go from day to night in that outfit, just add jewelry.

While we're on the topic of clothing, The Goodwill, Salvation Army, consignment shops and tag sales, are all great when you're looking for clothing or anything else for that matter.

When the U.S. went into an all-out recession in 2008, it changed people's shopping habits and these kinds of stores became the new trendy places to shop. Truth is, my family has always shopped at these kinds of places for this or that. You never know what you'll find there. When I am lucky enough to get together with my siblings, we hit these stores for fun. We fan out and go into hunting mode. The four of us know how to take something, no matter what it is, and turn it into something cool. We love this kind of treasure hunt.

Over the years my sisters, Carol (the teacher) and, Sue (the children's librarian) have bought hundreds of books at secondhand places to take into the classroom and library. My brother (who loves historic preservation) finds items to put in his home. My biggest find to date were bolts of high-end drapery fabric. I turned them into curtains in my home. That sewing skill I picked up as a kid comes in handy. Speaking of sewing, does anybody know how to do that anymore? You know, buy a pattern, lay it out on fabric and make a dress or skirt or curtains out of it?

We have taken life skills out of the public school curriculum. This is a huge mistake. If you want your children to learn how to sew, bake or work on cars, you either have to teach them yourself or pay to enroll them in classes outside of school.

My late father-in-law, Emil, was a shop teacher. I used to listen to his stories about teaching students to be carpenters and to weld and fix cars. At his wake, guys came into the funeral home telling my husband, Mark, about all the things they learned from his father and how they turned those skills into their life's work to earn a good living.

It's okay to be different; you might just start a trend.
—Ann Nyberg

My Rag Doll, "Shortie"

The older you get, the more things from your past mean to you, at least to me, anyway. My rag doll, "Shortie," falls into that category. I have no idea why I named her that but it stuck. My grammy Waggoner made her for me. She resides in a place in my closet where I can readily see her. She represents my childhood. I know what kind of love went into making her. She was held by the two hands of someone who is now gone. I am a sentimental fool, always have been, and that is why the past is so very important to me.

Grammy made a ton of these dolls for all of her granddaughters, as well as for a lot of little girls she didn't know. She was a churchgoer. Epworth Memorial United

Methodist Church figured into her life in a big way. She used to make lots of items for the church bazaars.

The "Shortie" dolls were stuffed with rags or nylon stockings in those days—five and six decades ago. My doll is more than 50 years old. One of her arms is missing, as is much of her once-braided hair, but she remains dear to me all the same. My grandmother embroidered her mouth and her eyes. The threads are, of course, worn but none of that matters.

Hours and hours of work went into, Shortie. Because I sew and knit, I understand how those hours of work turn into days. My mom still has the pattern for, Shortie. I'm sure she even gave me a copy, but I just haven't gotten around to making the doll.

While my grammy made my doll on her own, she used to come together with relatives and friends and make other things too; mostly quilts and other kinds of dolls. Women learned a lot from each other when they spent time together crafting. Back then, most families only had one car and women were home cooking and cleaning and raising the little ones.

I suppose this same kind of camaraderie happens in the book clubs that are so popular these days. Dolls aren't being churned out there, but friendships are being made, which is pretty darn important. The right kinds of friends make life beautiful.

Life moves pretty fast, and in my opinion we're losing sight of living in the "now." We're missing so much by not taking stock of what is around us. All of us gotta go, go, go, go. Where exactly are we all headed? We're all rushing, and technology is proceeding at such a break-neck pace that we can't even stay current with it. We're feeding and watering our online platforms daily, telling people what we're doing, where we're going. We're not even enjoying the moment because we're too busy trying to document it. What would happen if a big bad technology monster dropped out of the sky and ate up all our electronic devices and they were just gone in an instant? I can't even imagine the kind of 12 step programs we would have to put ourselves in. Unplugging? Have a conversation? What is that?

I am guilty of grabbing on to the next big thing to stay current. As a reporter, that's the deal. I want to stay current with the "Millennials" so I don't look ridiculous when my kids are trying to talk to me about this blog or that Instagram photo, and on and on and on.

I love writing about small business, innovators, entrepreneurs and things I find interesting. Thus, I founded NetworkConnecticut.com. I also own Annie Mame, a shop within a shop located in Madison, Connecticut where I love to sell goods made in the state. It helps push people forward. So that's two websites and then, of course, there is my Linkedin page for my resume and my Pinterest page for all the photos I collect for my DIY ideas. Oh, and my Facebook page and my Twitter account for all breaking news and it goes on from there. We're all connected everywhere, so now what? It makes us feel good that we know everything about everything but in the end what does that mean? Again, connected but disconnected from many things we need to be noticing right in front of us.

As much as I live in the "now," it is the past that gives me pleasure. I don't know, is it just my imagination that things were made to last longer decades ago? Cars and appliances and furniture and even my Shortie doll stood the test of time. Grammy's handmade stitches were so close together, a machine could have done the work. But that wasn't how she did it, her hands created something special, stitch by stitch.

I care deeply about my loved ones and I cherish the things I own that have memories attached to them. I don't know what will happen to Shortie as the years wear on. I'd like to think that people and wonderful places and things last forever, but they just don't. I hate that about life. Letting go is something I am just not good at but it happens, so make the most of wonderful things that are right in front of you.

Tokens of the past, don't take them for granted.
You held on to them for a reason.
—Ann Nyberg

Don't Waste
One More Sunset

The sun comes up and it goes down every day. How often do you take a moment to watch a setting sun, experience the ending of a day, ponder how you spent the hours or what might be on the horizon for you tomorrow? Most of us probably notice this kind of thing while we're on vacation or perhaps on a weekend in the summer, if we're near a beach.

My husband, Mark, tries to never miss a sunset, ever. He has made it a point to watch as many as possible from anywhere he is. He will rush to make it just in time to see the bright orb sink into the horizon. He has seen the sun set from many places around the world with me and without. He loves the moon too, but it's the sun that's highest on his watch list.

Countless stories and poems and songs center around dusk and dawn and the moon up above. Why is that?

I have had the amazing good fortune to travel over the years. There's nothing like travel to take in other cultures and to see how others live.

In my 40's, I went with my husband, who is a Professor of Medicine in the Yale University School of Medicine, to a scientific conference in the Aegean Sea. We were on the Cycladic island of Santorini. I had no idea what I was in for in that part of the world. That trip changed me forever. There aren't many days when I don't think about that volcanic island. There is nothing like this place on earth. Romantic doesn't even begin to describe it. If you're in love with someone, take them there! Make it a "must." There is a reason why there are at least 1,000 weddings a year there during the summer months.

By September, most of the tourists are gone and you have paradise that is much easier to see and experience. On this island, people come together on a ledge near the ruins of a mansion every night to watch the sun go down. It's beyond magical. The sun looks like it's on fire as it descends into the crystal blue Aegean. Every sunset is different, the colors of the sky change nightly. I have been to this island six times because it is so beautiful.

In the village of Oia, Kikladhes, a hotel called Canaves Oia has become "our place." It is owned by the Chaldemenos family. A few years back, I spent a whole afternoon talking to Markos—one of the sons who runs the hotel—about its rich history. What the family has built on this island is stunningly beautiful. I have taken hundreds of pictures there, by day and by night. There is something about this hotel that is hauntingly romantic. If you go and are in love, you will see what I mean. I have studied all about the village of Oia and the island itself. Thanks to Markos, Mark and I have sailed around this island too. What an amazing adventure on a catamaran. We shared the boat with a newlywed couple from Bulgaria. We lunched with them onboard and docked to have a swim in a very warm sulfuric cove. Imagine that? Talk about memories. I shot a video of this sail and posted it on YouTube just so I could always remember that day.

There are many who believe the buried city of Atlantis is at the bottom of the ocean there. Much of Santorini fell into the sea in 1410 during an enormous volcanic eruption, one of the largest in recorded history. This was at the height of the Minoan civilization. The eruption left a large caldera. That momentous event was followed by a giant tsunami that rolled all the way to the island of Crete to the south. Before you get on the plane to go there, you should read all about the island's history; it is truly fascinating. Santorini continues to rock and roll with much smaller earthquakes, which is what makes the place so exciting.

On one side of the island, there are "little white houses." They are caves—homes built into the side of the cliff overlooking the caldera. Millions of photos have been taken of this place; Google it and you will see. I describe the view of these caves as white frosting dripping down the side of a hot chocolate layer cake. To walk on the narrow streets so high up is exhilarating. It is impossible to take any bad photos on this island. The bright luscious fuchsia bougainvillea drips off the sides of the bright white homes in the sunset and nearly blinds you in the summertime.

There is a red beach on this island because of the eruption and a black beach. The black beach glitters; I think it is pieces of mica that catch the sun's light.

I have wanted to write a book about my adventures there. For 14 years or so, I have written about Santorini on napkins, notebooks and scraps of paper. Some of those words have found a home here. I was getting worried that all of that might not find its way into something permanent, where others could learn about the island. To say that I have a passion for this place and the Canaves Oia Hotel is a complete understatement. Never in my life did I think I would ever go to a Greek island let alone fall in love with one. Life does hand you surprises. It is here that I have spent beautiful moments with my husband and eaten amazing Mediterranean food. Ah, yes, and had white wine from grapes grown in nests on the sandy ground. It is very windy on the island so this way the grapes are nurtured and survive well. Think about that for a moment grapes grown on vines made into a nest.

The point to all of this—the trips, the sunsets, the people you meet—is about living a full life, making the most out of every day and not wasting time. It's about actually making time for a lot more trips and sunsets. When you travel, you learn so much about yourself and others.

The sun is setting. Are you watching?
—Ann Nyberg

Make Your Life Count

I sound like a broken record. I say this to myself and to others all of the time: "Make your life count, NOW!" You can't live your life as if you're rehearsing for the real thing. You have to live in the moment, find your passions and live them out. Surround yourself with people who will help you out when you need them.

Learn how to have fun, every day. Take a moment to go somewhere else in your head. You can still work when you're doing this, it just makes for a more pleasant day. The older I get, the more I start looking at my life in the rearview mirror and thinking about all the things I have done and the places I have been and where I will go in the future. I am not one of those people who just sits around, but I am mindful to be better about stopping and looking around and taking things in instead of missing out.

One of the ways I stopped the crazy routine of my life was to sit down and write a book. To put some thoughts down on paper. I will tell you, anyone who sits and toils over words and paragraphs and tries to make sense out of it all deserves an incredible amount of respect. Writing a book is very hard work. I have the utmost respect for authors and publishers and editors—anybody who champions the written word. So, go ahead and do something you've never done before, step out of your comfort zone.

Sarah Rose, my oldest twin daughter (by five minutes) had known for a long time that she wanted to live in the nation's capital. Guess where she ended up in her young twenties? She lives in Washington, D.C. Sarah is a no-nonsense-kind-of-gal who goes after what she wants. She loves books and has read all kinds of biographies about strong women. Someday, she may be in such a book. I can't wait to see where she lands in her career. I hope she is a leader so that others can follow her.

Don't look back and say to yourself, "If only I had done this or that". Just do it. None of us knows what is around the corner. I will share a story with you that stopped me dead in my tracks. As I was wrapping up this book, I ran into a woman in line at a Dunkin' Donuts. We had met years earlier at my house. She greeted me with a "hello" and we got to talking about the time she and her "tween" son had come over. We got our coffee and wrapped up our conversation and said goodbye to each other. I asked her to give my regards to her son from me. She stopped and said, "He passed away a few years back." She started to tear up. Though I was in a hurry, I stopped and listened to her.

She told me he died from a rare type of cancer. She went on to tell me that she had also lost her husband and her brother. I didn't know what to say, but I told her she had my utmost respect for getting up in the morning and putting on a smile and going to work. Life had handed her terrible tragedies.

My point of telling you this is that life is short—too short for some. Don't wait to do something that you want to do.

> *Life is fragile, hold every day dear.*
> —Ann Nyberg

Dogs Are People Too, Especially Savannah Jane

We're dog people—my family, my extended family, a lot of people we spend time with, are all dog people. Dogs just enrich lives.

The first dog Mark and I had in our married life was Pepsi, she was a Cock-a-Poo we got from the dog pound. We considered her our "starter" child. She started our married life with us and we moved her to Oklahoma where we lived for a few years and then brought her to Connecticut. Pepsi passed days before I delivered our twins. Lindsay, our oldest child, started her life with Pepsi.

There was some downtime in-between dogs after the twins were born. We were handling three children with no immediate family around and working. It was a lot.

When the time the twins were about twelve, Savannah Jane came into our lives. We had gone back to Indiana for Thanksgiving and returned to Connecticut with a 12 pound Labrador Retriever. We didn't have to buy her a seat; she fit nicely into a tiny soft bag on the plane.

Savannah Jane was like a sister to Lindsay, Sarah and Katie. She was raised with our kids, she was our kid. In many ways, she was all-knowing.

We lost her at age ten and the hurt still runs very deep. She just knew us all so well, every one of us. She knew when we felt hurt, she knew when we were happy. She was our girl. Her last trip in the car was to our cottage in Michigan. We didn't know at the time how sick she was. Sure, she was slowing down, but we had no idea what was coming. I think all of us were in denial that she would ever leave us.

In August of 2012, we were all together at the cottage with Savannah Jane, the twins, Lindsay and her husband, Paul. We all got to enjoy those last pontoon boat rides with our "Nanna." Savannah Jane had a ton of nicknames. Funny how that happens with pets. Each one of the kids called her something different. When it came time to get on the boat, she would run out on the pier. She never wanted to be left behind. She motored about with us on the lake, round and round. She went for swims with us too. When we anchored out in the middle of the lake, she swam in a life jacket.

A few shorts weeks later, she would leave us. We had to make that decision for her. She had started to suffer. That was a gut wrenching decision. Dogs don't tell you when they're in pain; they just wag their tail and are seemingly happy. But she had heart disease and we were told she had cancer too.

From her infancy, Savannah Jane carried around a stuffed white whale that was about twice her size. She loved that toy. The whale went everywhere with her and even to the cottage. That last trip, she slept on the whale a lot. (Perhaps it was security for her as she wasn't feeling well.)

Swimming was a huge part of her life, both in the lake and in our backyard pond. She swam every day in the pond. Around and around she would go, several times a day when it was warm. One of her nicknames was "Esther Williams," after the 1940's movie star who starred in films featuring her swimming. Savannah Jane stayed wet for most of the summer, so we always had a towel at the back door to dry her off when she came inside.

On the day we knew it was time for Nanna to go to heaven, we took her for one last swim in Long Island Sound. We were all there together. A sadder day just doesn't exist for dog lovers. We all watched her swim— knowing it was her last swim. Just writing this, years later, makes me tear up. We were with her at the vet's office and comforted her as she passed. She crossed over to the "Rainbow Bridge" where pets go until it's time for you to see them again.

We did not know what to do with ourselves when we left her. Thankfully, our Katie did. She wanted to go buy plaster-of-paris right away and go return to the shore where Savannah had taken her last swim only an hour before. We did that. We got the plaster and hurried to that spot. We got out of the car and saw that her paw prints still existed in the sand on that chilly wind swept day. Katie mixed up the plaster with sea water and poured it over as many of the paw prints as we could find, we had to hurry as we didn't want to lose those last imprints of our little gal. With all the paw prints filled, we waited for them to harden and wandered aimlessly on the all-but-deserted beach. Katie kept testing the plaster with a stick so we knew when we could gather up all the molds and take them home with us. Katie knew these would be gifts for all of us. None of us knew that she took them to be framed for us. On Christmas morning she handed each one of us our special remembrance of Savannah Jane. The tears flowed easily that day because of Katie's thoughtfulness and because we missed our dog sitting with us near the Christmas tree. Savannah could unwrap packages. That year, we couldn't watch her do that.

Though I had found Savannah Jane as a puppy, fell in love with her, and refused to leave Indiana without her, Katie and Savannah Jane had a special bond. They spoke the same language and were always together. We think of our Katie as a kind of "dog whisperer." She just knows what animals are saying. We now have two dogs, Henry Watson (a rescued coon hound who was found roaming about New York City) and Mr. Trip Meeshu (a golden retriever). They are the best of friends and we love them, though Savannah Jane will forever be in our hearts.

Do yourself a favor and discover
the unconditional love of a dog.
—Ann Nyberg

Conclusion

Learn the ABC'S of Life

A NSWER the call. When you're needed, step up, even when you're not asked. Look around, there is someone who needs your help.

B E kind even when it's difficult. You have no idea what might be going on in a person's life. Put a smile on, it might help.

C ONCENTRATE on the task at hand and do it well. You'll learn from it and be able to teach others.

D ARE to think outside the box. Being a follower your whole life isn't healthy.

ENTICE others to follow their passions. Life is short and too many people waste time.

FLOWERS, pick them, send them, have them around you. It makes the world a happier place.

GIVE of yourself whenever you can. It teaches others how much you can accomplish when you do.

HURTFUL words do damage. Think before you speak.

INNOVATE. Life is not about standing still. You might just change the world while you're at it.

JUMP at the chance to roll up your shirt sleeves and do something out of the ordinary. Hard work is good for the soul.

KEEP striving to be better every day. Random acts of kindness will lead you in a good direction.

L OVE deeply, even when it hurts. You'll then find the true meaning of life.

M OMENTOS, tuck them away for yourself and the generations behind you. They'll help tell your life's story.

N EARNESS to family and friends will make you a more complete person.

O PEN your heart to those who don't ask.

P ROMISES, keep them. Too many people don't and that breeds disappointment.

Q UIET, be still sometimes and listen to the sounds around you. You'll be amazed at what you hear.

R IGHT the wrongs when you can. It will make a difference in your life and for those around you.

STOP complaining. Get your own house in order first.

TRAVEL everywhere. See as much as you can. It will help you understand the world and make you a more tolerant person.

UPWARD, it's a good way to go. Move past whatever has you stagnating.

VINTAGE, that's another word for the past. It's about history, learn it, embrace it. By-gone eras can teach us a lot.

WEEDS, appreciate them. To some people, Queen Anne's Lace is a weed. Have you ever seen anything more beautiful or delicate?

XYLOPHONE, get one and play it. You had one when you were a kid and sometimes it's just nice to be a kid.

YOU can move mountains, be a leader. Surround yourself with doers who can help you.

Z, it's an ending. Now, go find your beginning. Your story.

A Closing Note

Ellen, my eighty-year-old mother, was my editor on this book. She was 23 when I was born. She sat with a pencil and read every word of her eldest daughter's writings. I wanted her to keep me honest and make corrections. Over two days out on the back porch at our house, she read and penciled in thoughts in the margins. From time to time, she would just start talking about her life too. The words on these pages stirred her memory and that got the two of us chatting about things we would never have talked about before. We were mother and daughter alone together. It brought me back to times we shared in our backyard in Eagledale, Indiana making dandelion necklaces.

This book ended up giving me a gift, the gift of time alone with my mom. I will cherish those hours forever, watching her read my lines about my life as a child under her guidance.

Give yourself the gift of sitting down with your parents and get their stories. It will help you know who you are as a person.

The Album

My mother, Ellen.

My father, John.

Aunt Martha, Uncle Montie and Ellen.

My paternal grandparents, Hanna and William
and my dad and his sister, Adele.

The twins Martha and Ann
with my maternal grandfather, Chester.

My paternal grandmother, Hanna.

My kindergarten photo.

My diary and the first story I did
in television news in 1979 on film.

My rag doll, Shortie.

My first car, "Louise" and my sister, Sue.

My wonderful siblings, Carol, John and Sue.

Savannah Jane with her favorite baby, the whale.

Birch Lake cottage "Chaos."

My family Lindsay, Sarah, Mark, me and Katie.

Overlooking the village of Oia from Canaves Oia Hotel, Greece.

My mother, Ellen, at the age of 80,
editing my book.

About the Author

Ann Nyberg is an Emmy-nominated on air talent with over thirty years experience in television news. She has been a marquee anchor in Connecticut for over 25 years. Ann has interviewed leading newsmakers and entertainers such as Peter Jennings, Walter Cronkite, Barbara Walters, Ann-Margret, Don Imus, Michael Bolton, Art Carney, Julie Andrews and more. A visionary in the industry, Ann started Network Connecticut in 2011 as a means for connecting the state on multiple levels. She is also the founder of the Toy Closet Program at Yale-New Haven Hospital.

HOMEBOUND
PUBLICATIONS

Ensuring the mainstream isn't the only stream.

At Homebound Publications, we publish books written by independent voices for independent minds. Our titles focus on a return to simplicity and balance, connection to the earth and each other, and the search for meaning and authenticity. As an independent publisher we strive to ensure, "That the mainstream is not the only stream."

It is our intention at Homebound Publications to preserve contemplative storytelling. We publish full-length introspective works of creative non-fiction, essay collections, travel writing, and novels. In all our titles, our intention is to introduce new perspectives that will directly aid humankind in the trials we face at present as a global village.

So often in this age of commerce, entertainment supersedes growth; books of lesser integrity but higher marketability are chosen over those with much-needed truth but smaller audience. Here at Homebound Publications, we focus on the quality of the truth and insight present within a project before any other considerations.

WWW.HOMEBOUNDPUBLICATIONS.COM

CPSIA information can be obtained
at www.ICGtesting.com
Printed in the USA
FFOW02n2233061015
17395FF